Stylish Minds, Frugal Finds

The High Low Fashionista's Guide to Thrifting

TALIA LESLIE

To My Mother

Thank you for teaching me how to navigate the thrift store like a pro. I love you.

The definition of a "thrift store" according to Merriam Webster:

A shop that sells second hand articles, especially clothes, and is run for charitable purposes.

The definition of a "thrift store" according to The High Low Fashionista:

A store where you can purchase one of a kind items at low prices. A place where creative shoppers can find high end items at a fraction of the retail price.

A fashionista's dream.

Chapter 1

I'M YOUR NEW BEST FRIEND

I'm Talia named after Talia Shire, the actress that played Adrienne in the Rocky movies. So it's safe to say that my mom did it for the culture because 1) I love all of the Rocky movies and 2) I'm a true 80's baby. Additionally, I am a lover of vintage style and I am an avid thrift shopper. The best way to describe my style aesthetic is a combination of ladylike mixed with modern motifs. If Whitley Gilbert, Lisa Turtle or Hilary Banks would wear it, so will I. I'm not sure if that makes me a Southern Belle or a Hollywood Diva or if I land somewhere in the middle; but on any given day, you might find me in designer jeans and satin gloves! I loved watching television in the 90's and viewing their black girl magic. I always admired their style and would try to emulate them through my wardrobe, but truth be told, we didn't have any money! My mom was a single mother that worked as a custodian at the local middle school and also worked part time at the movie theater on the weekends. Spaghetti was the meal of choice multiple nights a week and to this day, I have a hard time eating it. My mom's top priorities were keeping a roof over our heads and keeping food on the table. Shopping at the mall didn't even make it on the list so my dreams of dressing like Lisa Turtle seemed to go out of the window. I am grateful for my mother's effort to keep us focused in life and to ensure that we were focused on the essentials in life. I am also appreciative of her tenacity because it was her ingenuity that led us into the thrift store and began this wonderful world of thrifting.

Thrifting wasn't always socially acceptable. Some believed that only "poor" people shopped at thrift stores; therefore, thrift stores separated classes of people. However, my mother was never bothered by what people thought of her. She knew she had to shop within a limited budget and she knew that the thrift store contained unlimited gems. She was a proud woman and her confidence led her to the thrift store. I can remember being a young girl in the thrift store with my mother, who wasn't just a single mother, but a single mother of three children. My mom was always fashion forward. I thank God everyday that I inherited her innate sense of fashion and also her love for a good buy. You could always count on the *Essence Magazine* coming to our house every month, even if she was struggling to keep us fed. After all, some things are worth a good splurge. We often found ourselves in a Goodwill or Salvation Army. Now don't get it twisted, we were always, clean, well put together and we were always cute. I would like to think *Essence* had a small part in keeping us up to date on the latest trends. We may have shopped in thrift stores for the majority of our clothing, but my mom had a real knack for mixing clearance retail finds with our thrifted wardrobe. As a child, I thought my mom was simply going to the store and "picking out clothes". What I didn't realize is that my mom was creating art and performing a skill set.

My mother was not only an expert buyer, she was a top stylist. There are countless times when my mother ensured that I turned heads at whatever occasion I deemed important at the time. One particular time in high school, I was preparing for my school's winter pageant. All of the girls competing for the title of Miss ARJ were in the mall shopping for their pageant gowns to dazzle on the stage. My mom had scoped a purple off the shoulder gown in one of her favorite thrift stores weeks prior to me wanting to participate in the winter pageant. When I came home excited about the upcoming pageant, she was excited to tell me about the purple gown that she had come across that would be great for the occasion. She went on to tell me that it was the perfect dress since it was purple, which was one of the school colors. She was excited. I, on the other hand, did what a normal fifteen year old girl would do…cry. I knew my friends at school were excitedly discussing their mall dresses and I wanted to be able to join in on the fun! I told my mom that I didn't want the purple dress. I wanted one of the smooth velvet numbers that was on trend at the time. I begged her not to go back to that store and to leave that old dress where it was. Mom being the mother that she was- a mother that didn't let her fifteen year old daughter tell her what to do- went right back to the store the very next day. The old, purple dress that was on the rack the previous week for sixteen dollars was now marked down to four dollars. You already know that the dress

Mom brought the dress home and presented it to me. Through tears and teenage whining, she made me try it on. The four dollar purple thrift store gown fit like a glove. The hideous dress that was in my head was no more. It was a mermaid fit with off the shoulder details. Iridescent buttons that glistened from every angle lined the back. This… Dress…Was…Fabulous! A friend of my mom's allowed me to borrow her jewelry after seeing the dress. The jewelry provided the perfect accessory, as they matched the buttons on the back perfectly.

The big night finally arrived! I stood out in my thrifted purple gown and felt like a million dollars. Not only did I feel good but I stood out because every other girl wore the same velvet dresses that I wanted to go to the mall and buy. My thrifted purple dress that my mom scored was a show stopper. I did not win the pageant. But let's be clear, the pageant was never about being best dressed, it was about raising the most funds. So maybe, I lost according to the judges' report, but in the area of being best dressed, I won that competition! I received so many compliments after the pageant. I looked over at my mom and she had that "trust me child" look on her face. From that point on, I listened to my mother's advice, well, most of the time. After that experience, my love for fashion really started to blossom. Before Pinterest, I found myself making my own fashion collages in school notebooks. I would cut out photos and create trend boards. I had ideas of what best to wear in what season and what looks were appropriate for what occasion. Thrift stores became my playground because they allowed me to be creative and not break the bank. As a professional adult, I can now afford to purchase retail, but I still love the thrill of the hunt in a thrift store. I am able to be a master at a game that has been well played for hundreds of years; and now, so can you.

For me, fashion is what you buy and style is what you do with it.

The High Low Fashionista

The High Low Fashionista came to life during one of my reality television binges. Don't judge me, we all have our guilty pleasures. I have to give credit to The Real Housewives of Atlanta's very own,

Phaedra Parks, who coined the phrase "high-low fashions." While on vacation with her housewife cast mates, Phaedra discussed her outfit, which consisted of Target clothing paired with high end designer items. It was then that I thought to myself, I am the queen of "high-low fashions!" I have been lucky enough to score some pretty amazing designer goods simply by making my rounds to consignment shops and thrift stores. I love to mix pieces to create looks that you may see in magazines or on television shows. Designer bags and shoes are my weakness so on any given day, you may find me wearing Christian Louboutin shoes paired with a $2.00 thrifted dress. This love of "high-low" fashion has been passed down to my daughter who currently allows me to be her personal stylist as long as it's a dress or skirt, of course. I love to create her wardrobe from a mixture of thrifted finds combined with a little bit of Walmart and Target. She's the perfect model for the eclectic world we live in everyday. My sense of high low fashion brings balance in my life and ultimately, I want to send the message to every woman that there are no specific rules to follow. Every budget can create an amazing wardrobe. Now, let me show you how.

Chapter 2

#THRIFTLIFE

While my mother introduced me to the #ThriftLife, I have to give some credit to my career choice for making me delve deep into the racks of my local Goodwill. I was newly graduated from college (shout out to Fort Valley State University), and I had taken a teaching position as a Preschool Special Education teacher. I really thought I had made it! I was so excited about getting my first paycheck in my new career! I had so many dreams and plans for that paycheck! I was going to travel. I was going to purchase new furniture for my newly purchased condo. I was going to head to Lenox Mall and add to my shoe collection. The possibilities were endless and life was moving full speed ahead and I was swarming in all things black girl magic when I signed my documents to begin my teaching career.

In those days, you had to call the automated system to check whether your direct deposit was in your bank account. Don't laugh; I'm sure a lot of you reading know exactly what I'm talking about because there was no banking app to check balances like there are now. I recall waiting until midnight to check my "big ballin" bank account only to be disgusted with the automated voice. You mean to tell me that I worked a full month for $1500?! That couldn't be correct! I called the bank again (nothing changed) and then called my mother at 1:00 in the morning, who laughed at me. Apparently, this was not a crisis. No, the district didn't make a mistake. "Talia, that's how much a first year teacher with a Bachelor's degree brings home." I couldn't help but think about my mother. She began as a custodian, then started substitute teaching and then she proved anything is possible when she put herself through school and eventually became a teacher. Her first paycheck was actually less than mine and she had three kids at home and I had none. My mom took care of herself, her three children and ensured that we were all clean, fed and she even managed to teach me lifelong lessons while shopping for our basic needs. As an adult, many people probably thought I spent my entire teacher's paycheck on clothing because my wardrobe was full of quality brands and top fashions. However, I was simply employing the tools my mother taught me. I was visiting consignment shops and thrift stores and making the most of my money. I was carrying a Louis Vuitton bag on a teacher's salary not because I had a "rich uncle," but simply because I had a well-kept secret…I was a thrifter.

When I reflect on my early days of thrifting, I have to wonder why I kept the secret for so long? In a moment of transparency, I truly believed that others would look down on me because I rummaged through used clothing. This was not the most glamorous way to source items. Most people in my circle are what I call true mall shoppers. They bombard Saks and most often, show up to events looking like twins. When I realized that I wanted one of

One must learn how to play the game before they can become a master at the game.

a kind pieces that fit my style, I started driving back to those thrift stores and attacking the racks heavily. With a new appreciation for my personal style aesthetic, I started to share where I would find items when people complimented me. "Oh you like this dress? I only paid $2.00 for it." When mouths would drop in disbelief, I knew I was in my very own fashion lane and I loved it. About eighty-five percent of my wardrobe has been sourced at a thrift or consignment store. A fact that previously brought me shame now brings me pride and I can't wait to show you how to navigate the thrift store like a professional.

But wait, the high low game must not be entered into lightly. One must learn how to play the game before they can become a master at the game. It's important to discuss what you must do, and not do, to prepare to hit the thrifting streets. Many may think that you just hop in your car and GPS your way to the neighborhood thrift store, but preparation is key! You must map out a plan. I have many years of experience in the thrifting streets and I still make it a point to map out a game plan before venturing off into thrift wonderland. Are you ready? Let's go!

Dress The Part

When headed out on your thrift trip, there are some important things to keep in mind when preparing for your treasure hunt. First, is attire. Just like you have to dress the part for an interview, you have to have the right outfit to conquer the thrift shop. Your thrift uniform usually consists of a pair of leggings, a fitted tank, a pair of socks, shoes that are easy to take on and off (i.e. slides) and a loose fitting sweater that can easily be taken on and off.

As a novice thrifter, I wore jeans on one of my very first thrifting excursions. I learned quickly that this was not a good idea. Jeans made it difficult to try on skirts and dresses. Some thrift stores do not have designated dressing areas so I wasn't always able to try on my clothing selections. With a thrifting uniform, you can practically try on items in the middle of the store if needed. It is possible to find an item that you may want to try on right away. If this is the case, you are able to slide those pants right on top of your leggings. Take off that sweater and slide on that newly found blazer over your tank. You don't ever want to be restricted to trying on your finds in a thrift store. Undress and try on with confidence. I like to make sure that all items fit properly (more details on this in a later chapter). Your thrifting uniform will take the guess work out of correct sizing as vintage clothing often runs small. Labels cannot always be trusted and never be bound to a certain size. Use it as a guide. Try it on and if it fits, wear it! This helps to eliminate returns or taking home items that are not a good fit. The goal is to leave the store with useable pieces, not castaway items.

Choose The Best Location

This is the number one question from novice thrifters. When I started my Instagram page, The High Low Fashionista, I could count on followers jumping in my DM to ask where I shop or where they should shop in their area. I would simply share to begin at the neighborhood thrift store or chain stores such as Goodwill or Salvation Army. My reasoning is this: just because I posted a picture of a pair of Hermes sandals that I found at my local Goodwill, does not mean that you will pull up to the same store and score the exact same Hermes sandals. I instruct others to shop locally because this gives you the opportunity to do what I call "drop in shopping." There is a thrift store located near my job that I frequent often. I'm able to score great deals at this location because of the frequency of my visits and I bought the Hermes sandals during one of my "frequent" visits. Consistency is key and shopping local is best. I have found that loyalty, in any sense, always produces the best return.

Choose The Best Time

Yes, my friends, days and times play a key component in a successful thrift shopping excursion. I personally try to avoid weekend shopping if at all possible. Shopping on Saturdays and Sundays are usually the busier days for thrifting. New merchandise is not readily available on the weekends because 1) people clean out their closets on the weekends 2) people donate items on the weekends and 3) employees are not sorting and placing these items in the store on the weekends. So you guessed it, the weekend is the least opportune time to shop at a thrift store. The ideal time is to take a trip on Monday or Tuesday to check out the "new" offerings as the variety will be fresh and varied. Yes, even thrift stores have new inventory.

Make sure you are well aware of sale days. Just like retail, thrift stores need to constantly move inventory to make room for the new items that come in so they use the technique of the "sale" in order to move these items faster. Many stores have subscription lists so that you can be aware of when the sales take place so make sure that if you plan to visit the store frequently, you are a member of the list. Also, you should follow your favorite stores on social media to stay abreast of special sales and promotions they offer. In addition to sales, thrift stores use a color coding system to move their inventory and this is where you are really able to take advantage of your savings.

It is important to learn the color rotations to track sales in thrift stores. Goodwill stores use a color rotation system to clear out inventory. There are five different colors that are used. For example, new clothing that is rolling out on to the sales floor may be labeled with a blue tag. Next week's color of the week may be orange. On Sunday, Goodwill will put the oldest color tag on sale for 50% off in order to clear inventory fast and get ready for the racks of donations to roll out. If you can figure out your store's color rotation, this can give you an idea of when a particular item you spy may get an additional discount. Remember, there is a strategy and your job is to master the strategy.

Seasonal shopping is another important tip to keep in mind. Individuals are always cleaning out to make room for new items around the holidays. Families are visiting, kids are gearing up to receive new toys from Santa, and ladies, you know we are readjusting our closets to get ready for new items. This is prime shopping time to gather new housewares as well as fresh inventory to add to your wardrobe. The tax write off for the end of the year is a major driving force behind donations around this time. Summertime is also a great time to shop because families take this time to move. When moving into a new home, people take this opportunity to clear out the old to prepare for the new. Use this to your advantage to score big in the area of housewares and furniture.

As far as time of day, there is no best time to "pull up." There is no theory in telling an individual that 2:00 p.m. is the absolute best time to shop. I feel that the best time to shop is when the mood hits me. I have been driving down the street and will hear a little voice in my head telling me to stop or turn around and check out the thrift store I may have just passed. These types of trips do not happen often so please keep that in mind. Keep all of these things in mind when learning how to become a master in the world of thrifting.

Become A Thrift Store Pro

There is a certain way to move in the thrift store and there is such a thing as thrift store etiquette. There are a few stores that you may visit that you must know the rules in order to navigate the space. I'm not saying this to scare anyone. I just want you to be well aware of the thrift store gangsters that lurk the aisles. As a seasoned thrifter, there are some stores that I will not venture in on certain days. Those days include "All items are $0.50!" On those days, the shoppers can be ruthless and I'm not trying to catch a case for a $0.50 cent blouse. However, the rules below should help you become a responsible shopper and not catch a thrift store case!

Thrift Store Etiquette

Rule #1 - Respect the employees as well as other shoppers and their personal space.

Rule #2 - Don't takeover the aisles. Thrift store aisles are narrow and adding a shopping cart to that space can make for a tight enclosure. Make sure you are aware of other shoppers around you. Also, keep your shopping cart in close proximity to the clothing racks. Whenever you are in a tight space, smile and be kind to your fellow shoppers.

Rule #3 - Please don't lean on your shopping cart to take a break in the middle of the aisle. Move over to the side to avoid other shoppers if you need a rest. Trust me, a quick break is often needed.

Rule #4 - No loud talking on your cell phone. No one likes to hear your conversation while trying to focus in the thrift store. Please don't put your caller on speaker phone. I do not what to hear what Linda told Tonya to tell Marie. Please don't kill my "thrift" vibe. As a matter of fact, make this a rule for everyday life.

Rule #5 - Do not reach over someone or someone's shopping cart to get an item from a rack or shelf. Can you say, personal space ma'am? Just don't do this.

Rule #6 - Do not shop out of other people's carts, this will get you hemmed up! Trust me, I'm not a fighter; but this might make me lay the smack down. Keep your hands to yourself. You had the same opportunity to find the items that may be in someone else's cart. Finders keepers, losers keep searching the racks for your own gems. Remember, you came to find clothes, not to lose the ones you have on!

Rule #7 - Bring your own tote bag. Skip the plastic and help save the environment. In the words of Captain Planet, "The power is yours." Be kind to our planet.

Chapter 3

THE ROAD MAP TO FASHION

When you are thrifting, it's easy to overspend. The prices are super affordable so it can be easy to get to the cashier and have sticker stock. I will admit, I have been obsessive at the thrift store before and ended up with a $160.00 bill, along with a look of confusion. The cashier and I had a mini staring contest before I came to the realization that I needed to either pay up or put items back on the rack. I now have a process that I do to ensure that I am not met with any surprises at the cashier. Before getting into that process, I must stress the importance of setting your budget. When I shop in consignment shops or stores that have more high end vintage finds, I plan to have a larger budget to accommodate the pricing. When shopping in stores that have additional savings, I give myself a smaller budget. In all cases, I do my best to stay within the budget I have set.

There is a consignment shop in my area, Back By Popular Demand, that has a seasonal sale where every item is one dollar. You have to get up early in the morning to get in line for this sale, but it is totally worth it. Consignment shops have great selections because their items are hand selected by employees so you are guaranteed to find a few gems. When I attend the Dollar Sale, I make it a point to set my budget. I go to the bank and get cash to take with me. I don't want to be tempted by credit or debit card swiping. The last time I took advantage of the sale, I brought $30.00 with me. I tried with all my might to stick to the budget, but my shoes took me over budget by $2.00. Thankfully, I had a thrift sister, the administrator over one of the largest thrifting groups on FaceBook, loan me the extra $2.00 needed to purchase my Tory Burch sandals (they were priced out at $1.00 per shoe). This was one time it was necessary to go over budget. It is important to set a budget and stay in budget. This is a process that gets easier as you continue thrifting and building your wardrobe.

This last tip does not always work, but never be afraid to ask for an additional discount. I always carry my teacher identification and for a long time, I carried my college student identification. If you are a member of the military, ask if they offer a discount. Whenever I shop with my mom, I ask if the store has a senior citizen's discount. By the way, this is about the only time my mother is ok with being identified as "old." (Insert Eye Roll)

Thrift Wish List

Manifest those thrifted finds, Sis! Do you want a designer bag? Write it down! Having a list will keep you focused on your goal. Every girl should have a thrift wish list, both short term and long term! I have been lucky enough to manifest a few items on my list, like my Chanel bag and sequined blazers. There are still a few things that I am currently on the hunt for and I realize that it may take a while for them to magically turn up in my local thrift store. I am ok with the wait because I know that the Thrift Gawds are always looking out for your girl!

A Beginner's Thrift Wish List:
1. Little Black Dress
2. Black Tailored Blazer
3. Denim Jacket
4. Unique Vintage Belt
5. A Classic White Shirt
6. Dark Denim Jeans

As you get comfortable navigating the thrift store, your list will begin to get more specific. Building a wardrobe from this list will allow you to stay focused on key pieces while on your treasure hunt.

Thrifting Tool Kit

There are items that I always come armed with in my cross body bag (remember this from Chapter 1). When I thrift, my adrenaline runs high and it feels like I am running a 5K (yes, calories). I always carry a small bottle of water along with a light snack such as a granola bar

My Thrifting WISH LIST

NOTES

(yes, snacks). It is easy to go through racks of items and then realize you need a break to eat or drink. Keeping light items such as the aforementioned will provide the proper nourishment so you won't be passed out in the thrift aisles.

Sanitize those hands! Having a few pairs of gloves and hand sanitizer will give you protection as you sift through racks of clothing. There are thrift stores that are pay by the pound and they will roll out huge bins of items that you must go through to find those diamonds in the rough. You will want to wear gloves, especially if you are adventurous enough to explore one of these types of stores. I can recall going to a "bins" store in Savannah and was freaked out when I came across a dead bug in the bins. Let's just say, I haven't been back to one of those types of thrift stores again, but should I decide to ever go, I am armed and ready with sanitizer and gloves.

This next tool is something that I'm sure you won't leave home without, but I want to share how to utilize it as a thrifter. When thrift shopping, I always make sure that my smart phone is fully charged. I do this, not because I like to take pictures of magnificent finds, but because I like to do a quick search on unfamiliar brand names. Unfamiliar brand names are often Googled to see when it was manufactured, where it was manufactured and if the brand is still in production. It is also interesting to find brands that are sold exclusively in select department stores. I have had to conduct numerous Google quick studies and I am always fortunate when I find unique brands or pieces. If an item is in great condition, I have Googled to see what the retail price was or whether or not I'm familiar with the brand. While thrifting in San Francisco, I came across a beautiful black coat that had a unique latch detail on the shoulder. Upon Googling the brand, All Saints, I discovered that this jacket was an $800.00 coat that I found for $3.99 at the Salvation Army. Talk about a score! I was so excited to pack that coat up and bring her home. It was actually the best part of my trip!

Consignment Shops vs. Thrift Stores

I've said it before, but I'll say it again- thrift stores are hidden gems. I have been lucky to find some fabulous pieces, some so awesome that no one believes that I got it from a thrift store. Although I have friends that often beg me to take them with me on my treasure hunts, I know that they are not about that thrift store life! Most do not understand that sometimes you have to dig through piles of clothes to find that Prada skirt that you may see hanging in my closet. Thrift stores can be unorganized and flat out dirty and I know who I can and cannot take with me to these places. I do not need a turned up nose stopping me from the hunt. It kills my vibe and my vibe must be alive if I'm going to find the next great buy.

So let's discuss the difference between thrift stores and consignment shops. There are parallels, but also some major differences between the two. Thrift stores may vary. There are Goodwill and Salvation Army stores that are on the popular end of the spectrum. These stores are donation based and generally focus on charity or helping others in the community with job skills and aid people with disabilities (which is near and dear to my heart as a special education teacher). People in the community donate used goods to these organizations. Clothing, shoes and home goods are processed to sell. The workers there sort and organize items so your local Goodwill may be pretty well organized and easy to navigate. I, however, enjoy thrift stores that are off the beaten path. I have found some of my most unique pieces in the grimy, smelly, non-traditional thrift stores. Don't be afraid to dig through a pile of rags! The adage "never judge a book by its cover" is certainly true when it comes to thrift stores. Never dismiss a store because of its appearance. If you know what you are looking for, this is where the real jewels are!

For my bougie crew, the shoppers who I know cannot handle a traditional thrift store, I suggest consignment shops. There are several models of this type of resale shop. Consignment shops have staff with well-trained eyes. Buyers that are employed in consignment shops evaluate items for any rips, tears, missing buttons, broken zippers, etc. Let's just say the item has to be in great condition. Not only does it have to be in good condition, the item must be in season. Buyers take all of these factors into consideration when approving pieces to resale in their stores. If the item passes the test, the shop sales the item on behalf of the owner while taking a percentage of the sales price. It is normally a 40/60 split (the owner receiving 40% while the consignment store keeps 60% profit). Some consignment shops will pay the sellers when their items sale while others like Plato's Closet will offer cash up front for your items. Consignment shops are well organized and offer the current trends of the season. I will often shop consignment if I am in need of a specific item such as new shoes or a dress to wear to a wedding. If I'm not in the mood to hunt for an item, consignment is my go to resource.

If you are looking for an item on demand, I will let you know right now, the thrift store nor the consignment shop should be your first stop. Let's just say you are looking for a black jumpsuit for an event you are attending tomorrow night. Go ahead and head to the mall, Sis.

Thrift stores are difficult stores to find items on demand. They are inconsistent and unpredictable and just outright random! I can recall purchasing an evening gown on one of my random drop-ins after school. I remember feeling like I struck gold! It was a beautiful turquoise one shoulder beaded evening gown. At the time, I had nowhere to wear it and it hung in my closet for years. That dress finally got to see the light of day when my girlfriend invited me to the Mayor's Ball in Atlanta, Georgia. I rocked that $5.00 dress with the best of Atlanta on that night! There will be times when you find a piece in the thrift store and it will take weeks, months, or in my case, years to make its debut. Trust me, if the garment is fabulous enough, it will be worth the wait!

Labels, Labels, Labels

I'm not afraid to admit that I love labels! I have been lucky enough to find designer labels such as Chanel, Louboutin and Prada in the thrift store. The key to this is not looking for it. I don't walk in the store and say, "Today, I'm looking for a Louis Vuitton bag." Of the times I've scored designer finds, it has been on a day where I have popped in looking for nothing in particular, which in my case is most days. The trick to finding those great designer pieces is knowing how to identify plush leather goods and well made items. A lot of times, the items in the store will not be logo heavy so it wont jump out and scream, "I'm A Gucci bag!" If I'm being truthful, the knockoffs are usually the items that the thrift stores over price and the unassuming pieces are put out with the regular handbags. This is when you will use your keen eye to search for those quality/ well made pieces. Now if you are in the market for a pair of designer shoes or a handbag, check out your high end consignment stores. Sellers take items to these resale shops to offload their unworn items. Remember, thrifting requires strategy and you are improving your strategy with every visit.

Hanger Appeal or Nah?

When strolling through the racks of the thrift store, you may find an item that may look unappealing on the hanger. If you are armed and dressed in your thrifting uniform, you can easily try on that item and see if it has potential. In order to be a great thrifter, you have to come armed with imagination. It's important to look beyond the hanger when examining the next great buy. Clothing can often times be deceiving when you pull it off the racks. For my novice thrift besties, be sure to try on items because vintage items run smaller than tagged. I like to try on all potential items because you may miss out on a jewel by just simply checking the size. I once purchased a size 14 dress that I wore as a duster and I received lots of compliments on that vintage piece. As a thrifter, you are also becoming a stylist. You will soon realize that many pieces can have multiple purposes if you allow your imagination room to grow beyond the hanger.

When scanning racks, it is important that I touch every article of clothing on the rack. For a new thrifter, this may be a tedious task. I have mastered the scan and touch, and I will help you do the same effectively by giving you a few tips.

I tend to scan by color and print. I focus on pieces that are visually attractive to me. I will admit, I'm partial to pink so a lot of my personal selections are pink. I'm also partial to color, so even if it's not pink, it is definitely colorful. I am a fabric feeler. This will give you an idea of the quality of the article. This is key when thinking about comfort and wearability. Try to stay away from nylon and polyester, as some of those materials tend to give off "cheap" vibes, and ladies we don't want that look, ok! Just because we are getting a great deal doesn't mean we are cheap. There is a huge difference.

Check the tags. This is your time to be a label whore. This part gives me all of the feels! There is nothing like coming across a high end brand for the low. If the store tags are still attached, this is definitely a bonus!

Before making your way to the cash register, double back to the fitting room. No, I'm not telling you to try on everything again. As an experienced thrifter, I will always sort through my items and put back items in the fitting area racks. People, this is your opportunity to score big without having to hunt down items. Shoppers always leave items that may have not worked for them. Be sure to check out those pieces because they may work for you. I love putting together outfits only to leave them hanging so that a lucky person will run across it and purchase it. I have nicknamed myself the fairy thrift mother! Who knows, you may come in a thrift store after me and discover one of my special surprises! Consider it my gift to the world (along with this book)!

Perfecting Your Shopping Cart

I've already mentioned that thrifting can feel like you are running a 5K race. When thrifting, it is important to grab items that speak to you at that very moment. You may not have the opportunity to back track to get that particular article of clothing that you saw five seconds earlier. It's real in these thrifting streets! You will not have time as you are sorting through racks to carefully analyze each piece. If an item is hanging on the hanger, it is fair game! Do not let another thrifter snatch something right up under your nose. Believe me when I say that they will if you are not moving fast enough. I call the method that I use "the grab and roll." If I see an item of interest, I place it in my shopping cart. This allows me to keep moving to cover more thrift territory. I will warn you, this method will have your cart overflowing with items. It is then that I start the editing process. I find a section of the store with minimal traffic and room to accommodate an additional shopping chart. If the area has a mirror, that is a plus! I will then sort through each article with my detective's eye. I will inspect for stains, rips and other damage. This is the time to try on the garment and test the zippers to ensure they are functional. Because you are in your thrifting attire, you will have no problem trying on items. Hanger appeal is real so it is important to try on your clothing. A lot of thrift stores do not allow you to return items so you want to be sure that items selected are quality pieces that fit well and have minimal to no damage. Don't be afraid to change your mind. You picked up items in the thrill of the chase. Now, you remaking wise choices before you buy. You want to make sure that you are happy with everything that you purchase. Inspect. Filter. Buy.

Chapter 4

INSPECTION LEADS TO PERFECTION

You know what burns my biscuits? Getting your fabulous new item that you just scored and prepping to wash, only to find out that it is missing buttons or the zipper doesn't work. This my friends is when you start questioning your thrift skill level. We don't want to have to spend too much money repairing an item so let's do as much inspection as possible inside of the store. Let's take a look at each type of apparel so you can be prepared before you go to the store.

Shoes- Since the shoe section is one of my first stops on my thrift store map, I want to start here to let you know how to carefully inspect footwear. Always carefully inspect the sole and heel to make sure that both are in tact. There is nothing like wearing a pair of shoes and the heel breaks as you are strutting your stuff! Check the tap of the shoe as well as any damage on the heel. These can be easily fixed if the shoe is worth taking it to a good cobbler. The inside of the shoe should also be assessed for anything suspicious looking.

IMPORTANT NOTE: MOLD or anything that looks like it will cause your toes to have to be amputated. If you don't believe that disinfecting the shoe will work, leave them there, Sis. No brand or look is worth an infection.

Tops- When looking at blouses or shirts, the first area I check is the arm pit areas. If they are stained, it's a no for me. More than likely, the stain couldn't be removed or the previous owner was not the most sanitary. Be sure to check the front of your tops for stains. You have to closely inspect these areas. You know how food drips on the front of your shirt when eating? Oh, just me? Ok. Also, make sure to check the sleeves for stains, especially around the wrist area. Missing buttons are not always a deal breaker, just make sure you are aware of any missing buttons for the front or back closure and sleeves.

Pants- Thanks to my thrift outfit, I have the ability to try on pants in the store. I always check for functional zippers. Be sure to check for missing buttons or clasps. The most important area to check on pants is the crotch. This will determine if the pants make it to the cashier. Not only will you be checking for stains, you will need to check to see if the area where the thighs meet are worn thin. Lastly, check for rips in the seams and hems.

Handbags- When pulling a handbag, my first area of inspection goes into the initial front visual of the handbag. Are there any obvious stains on the front or back? Any holes or rips? The handles on purses are usually the first place to show extensive wear. Be sure to check for fraying or discoloration in this area. Once the outside inspection is complete, I then check the interior lining for stains and tears. The hardware is the last stop on my inspection. Check zippers and any hardware to be sure that it is in working order.

Sweaters- When looking at sweaters, check for what I like to call fuzz balls or pilling. If there is a lot of fuzziness, the item may be beyond repair and alerts me that the wear on the item may be too much for me to try to salvage. When inspecting vintage and I discover fuzz monsters, I usually leave the pieces behind.

Embellished Items- Who doesn't love finding pieces with sequin or appliqué detail? These pieces, especially vintage, have to be inspected closely. Be sure that all beading or sequin is in place. A few missing sequins or beads are not a total deal breaker; however, if I purchase items with missing beads or detail, it need not be noticeable. It is important to look for the source of where the sequin is missing to avoid any other pieces unraveling. You do not want to be that girl that leaves a trail of your sequined dress wherever you may go!

Proper inspection in the store prevents future disposal at home. Check it twice!

Leave that in the store, Sis!

I am all about the #thriftlife, but not every item can be bought at the thrift store or the consignment shop. The following items listed are things that don't make it to Chateau Leslie.

Car Seats- I see quite a few car seats on my thrift trips. Car seats are designed to withstand only one crash. How do you know if it has been in an accident? You don't! Leave this item where it is and keep the kiddies safe.

Swimwear/underwear- I shouldn't have to get too deep into this so here it goes…Yuck!! That's disgusting! Undergarments in the thrift store scream "Stranger Danger!" Now, there was a time that I found a few Victoria's Secrets bras that were new (still with tags on) that I did purchase, but that was an exception. I broke my own rule here to save myself $58.00; but, I repeat- they were NEW and STILL HAD THE TAGS! There are exceptions to the rule and this was one of them. But in 2020, we are leaving the new undergarments in the store too.

Makeup- Makeup doesn't last forever. Eye makeup, such as mascara and liquid eyeliner, should be replaced every three months. Once you open makeup, you have started the breeding ground for a bacteria party if brushes and applicators are not sanitized correctly. That tube of mascara you found in the beauty section of the thrift store needs to stay in the bin you found it in. The product could be aged and the previous owner might not have been sanitary. Head on down to Sephora and purchase your new makeup. Trust me on this one.

Plastic Containers- These items absorb smells and stains. Containers are fairly inexpensive down at the local Walmart so let's make sure we remove this from the thrift list also.

Worn out shoes- I look at some shoes and think even the best shoe cobbler can't save these! Leave those broke down shoes where they are. Your feet will thank you.

Metal and Nonstick Cookware- The coating on nonstick pans break down over periods of time. They then release chemicals that can be harmful and I'm positive you don't want those problems.

Things that cost more than their retail price…Believe me, those items are out there. When I see overpriced items in the thrift store, I can't help but think that the employee was super proud of the particular item when they were tasked with pricing. Please be aware that some thrift stores have "special pricing" for designer items that may land in their donation bin. This is where you must know as a consumer how to gauge retail prices. Google is your friend! Take the time to check pricing so that you won't be paying $20.00 for a dress that actually costs $10.00 at Target.

There are some items that have to be bought at Walmart or Target. Your safety and well-being demand it. However, you can conquer those stores, also. Take the strategies you're learning here and employ them at the big box stores. You've got this!

The same applies to thrift store employees and regular shoppers.

"A man that hath friends must shew himself friendly…" Proverbs 18:24

Good friends are like black dresses. They never go out of style…so keep a few in stock! Because I frequent the Goodwill location by my school regularly, I have come to know the workers and frequent shoppers by first name, and if I don't…I at least act like I do! It pays to be nice. I believe this mindset comes from my days of working retail. I remember being excited when my regular customers came in and I really enjoyed building those relationships. It makes shopping fun and it can be beneficial in the thrift shop. One particular day, I stopped by the thrift store on my way home from work. This wasn't a trip to decompress, but I was looking for a bench to set up a seating area in my hallway. I had looked online at all of the websites that sell furniture and did not want to drop over $200.00 on a bench that was simply for hall décor, and of course all of the ones I liked were pricey! Go figure!

Upon arrival, I bypassed all of the clothing, shoes and jewelry. These are typically the first stops on my treasure hunt, but today I was only concerned with furniture. I went directly to the furniture section, only to be disappointed! There was nothing! Friends, please keep this in mind- when you set out on your thrift trips, you may not find what you are looking for every time and it's ok! Accept this fact and hold on to this nugget. I turned in defeat, as I had no interest in clothing that day. As I walked towards the front door, a man almost ran into me with his shopping cart. Let's just call him George. He apologized for almost running me over. I accepted his apology and looked in his cart only to be mesmerized by the beautiful wooden bench hanging out of his cart. I then told George that he had beat me to the bench; I mean all is fair in thrifting. He got to it first so I had to suck it up and move on. As I turned to walk away, George told me that I could have the bench. I could not believe what I was hearing. He told me that he was only buying it because it was discounted 50% off, but it was just going to sit outside his home. I told George my plan for it and he was just as excited as I was about my home décor project and he wheeled it up to the cashier for me. I now had a bench that I had manifested for only $3.50. Thanks, George! Some may think George is my Thrift Angel and that I would never see him again, but I can count on seeing George and his buddy Charles in this Goodwill location every Wednesday around 4:00p.m. If I make a stop on that particular day, I know that they will be there to ask me how my day was at school. We chat about the newest finds- they both love gadgets- and we part. I have met so many interesting people at the many thrift stores I frequent. It feels like we are connected through our love of the treasure hunt.

People who know me, know that I am a people person and will take the opportunity to chat with just about anyone. Just as you may get to know the manager in your favorite boutique, or in my case, the girl in the shoe department at Nordstrom's near my house, I am sure to befriend the thrift store workers. Don't discount them as not knowing the inventory because they do. And when they see you enough, and know what types of items you are looking for, they will sometimes let you know about the Louis Vuitton bag that's in the back of the large haul of sunglasses that were donated that morning. These things have happened, and yes, I scored big on the sunglass haul. Can you say Tory Burch sunnies for $4.00?

Employees that work the floor are the best resource on your thrift hunt. At times, they may be busy, but if you smile and have a pleasant disposition, you may have a new thrift bestie with intel. Thrift store workers are one of the keys to my thrift success. Tap into the knowledge they have in order to be successful on your thrift trips. They spend more time inside of the thrift store than anyone else; why wouldn't you want them on your team?

Make friends, make moves. It's just another strategy in the game of thrifting.

Chapter 5

AN INTERNATIONAL PHENOMENON

Let me disappoint you. America is not the fashion capital of the world. Yes, Los Angeles and New York are fabulous, but the great fashionistas of the world are not American. Sad, I know. So what does this mean? If you think thrifting in America is great, then thrifting internationally is an art form.

It had always been a dream of mine to travel to Paris and emerge myself in the culture, namely, the fashion culture that France has to offer. My husband, knowing that Paris was on my bucket list, allowed me to plan our one year anniversary trip to Paris and once I was given the green light, I planned a trip of a lifetime along with a map of all of the must see thrift stores in Paris. As soon as we arrived, I grabbed my Rick Steves pocket guide to Paris and a French translation book, and we hit the ground running to explore all that Paris had to offer!

Thanks to social media, I learned my college friend, Paige, was in Paris at the same time so we decided to meet up and do some shopping. Paige's friend just so happened to be from Paris so he took us to all of the local spots- places that I did not find on my Google search! Our first stop was a flea market. We strolled up to this open market and all of the antiques and vintage items took my breath away! There were blocks of different vendors with beautiful and unique pieces. I had literally died and gone to heaven! I began to think about how I was going to get all of the items I wanted home. My husband just let me bask in all of the vintage glory. I picked up several vintage dresses and skirts, and most are still hanging in my closet today. I can honestly say, that thrifting in Paris has been one of my most memorable thrift trips to date.

On the date of our anniversary, my husband told me that he did not pack an anniversary gift. Although we were still in Paris, he still got a side eye from me. However, he went on to hand me a card with a handwritten note inside. The note said that he was taking me to

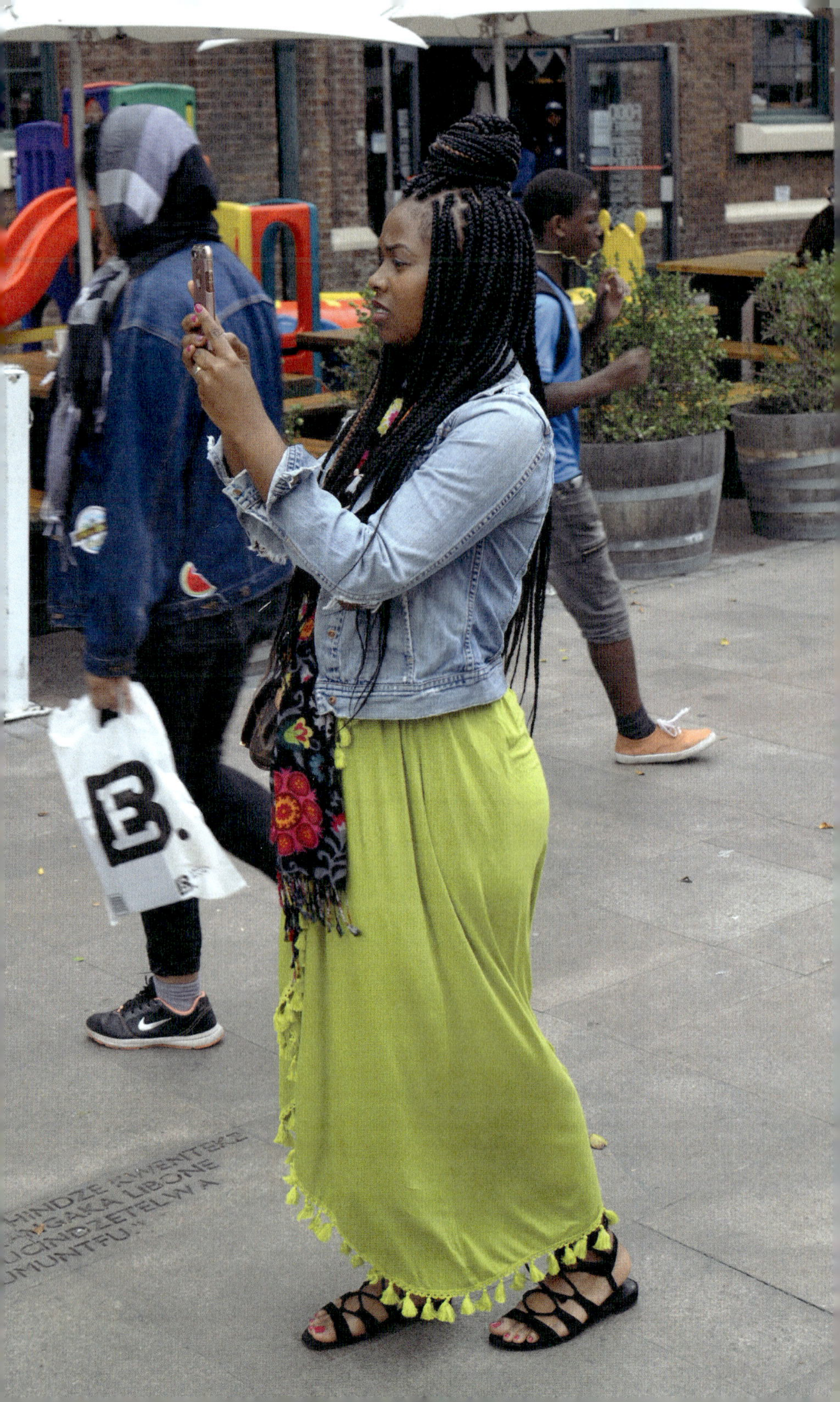
B.
HINDZE
LIBONE
UMUNTFU

41

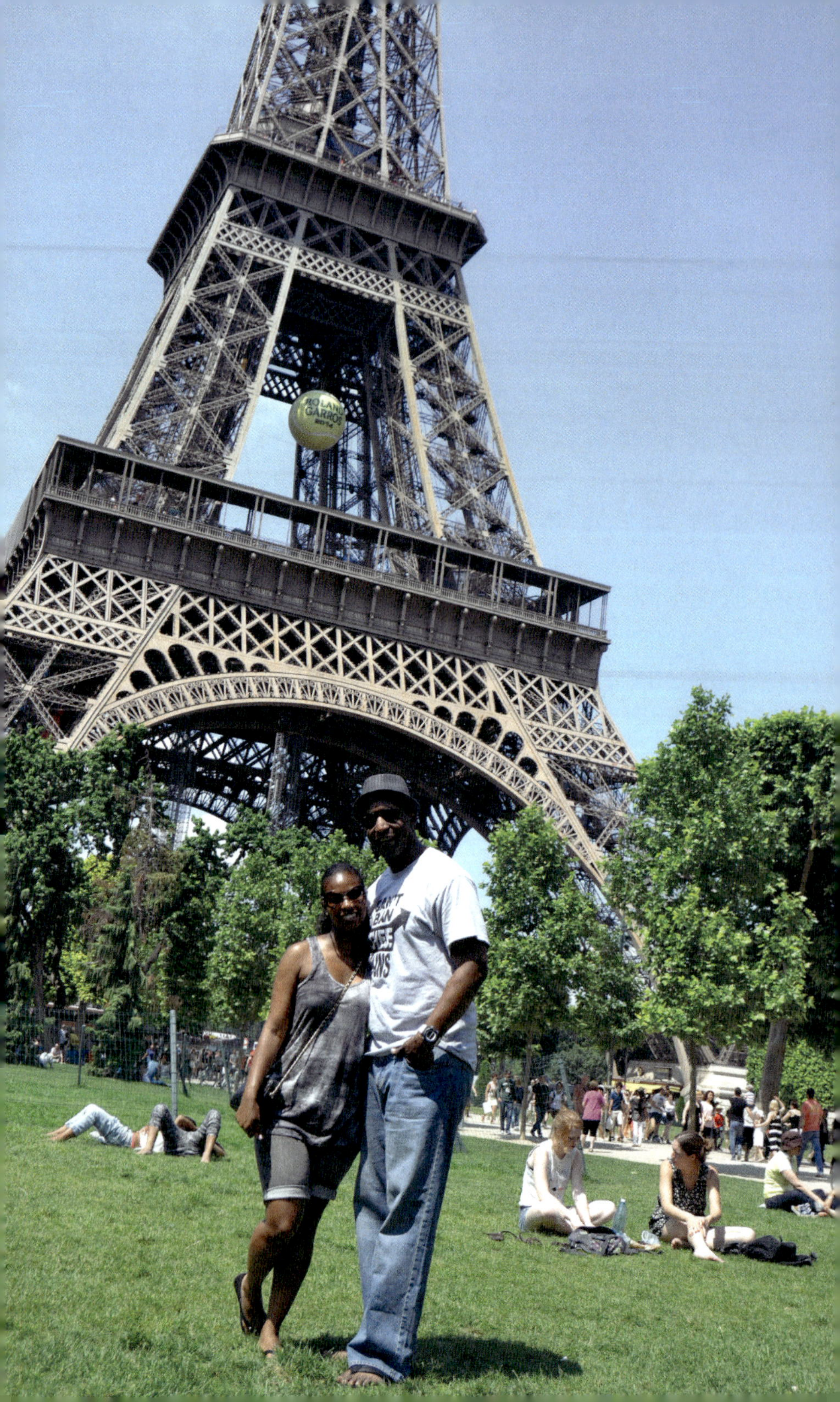
ROLAND GARROS

43

the Louis Vuitton store to purchase the handbag of my desire. Most women would have jumped at this offer, but not the self-proclaimed "Thrift Queen". I told him to give me the money and armed with my list of thrift and consignment stores, I set off to find a handbag at a fraction of what he would have paid at the Louis Vuitton store. And to answer the question I know you have, yes I found a vintage Louis Vuitton bag! Yes it is authentic and yes I saved hubby a few coins! Can you say, "Best Trip Ever?!"

Traveling=Thrifting

Wherever I travel, I map out the thrift stores where I would like to visit. I simply Google the stores and read the reviews for each store in order to compile a list. I have had the opportunity to thrift all over the country and all over the world, including the motherland of Africa. While Atlanta is my favorite place to shop, I have to give a shout out to California. San Francisco and Los Angeles are two of my favorite cities to shop. My family knows that I will have a dedicated day to check out the thrift stores while on vacation. Armed with Google, a plan and determination, I set off to explore. In order to get around town without inconveniencing my family, I will call a Lyft or Uber to chauffeur me to my thrifting destinations.

Thrifting in other cities and especially in other countries allows you to gain various fashion perspectives and take advantage of finds you wouldn't ordinarily have at your disposal. There are some designs that don't make it to the South so if you have a trip planned to the West Coast or to the North, take advantage of the moment and thrift away! Additionally, thrifting in other countries allows you to immerse yourself in the culture. When I traveled to Cape Town in South Africa, I allowed myself to become one with the people, the music and the food. Being able to shop and bring back items made the memory even richer. Thrifting in the motherland is an experience I will never forget. While I was able to obtain some authentic pieces, I also added to the cultural experience of a lifetime. Don't miss these moments.

Cleanliness before...Anything Else!

With over fifteen years of thrifting experience under my belt, I tend to think of myself as a chemist when it comes to cleaning and sanitizing items after being purchased in the thrift store. Here are a few items that I keep in my cleaning kit to ensure my items are clean and sanitized before wear.

Vinegar- Vinegar is a natural deodorizer. It's also a natural fabric softener. When cleaning thrifted clothing, it is important to add one half cup to your laundry to aid with disinfecting mold and mildew. Vinegar is also a natural alternative to bleach for brightening up those white items you may find! It won't harm your laundry machine so no worries, sanitize away!

Baking Soda- This can be used as a "laundry booster." Adding this to your washing machine aids in removing dirt from clothing. If you get an item home and notice it has a bad odor, add some baking soda to neutralize the smell. It turns out baking soda isn't just used to sit in the refrigerator!

Awesome Cleaner – This is a Dollar Store Purchase that gets out hard soiled areas. I always do a small test on the material first to be sure it won't be harsh on the fabric. Once it passes the test, go to work!

Items that are Dry Clean only are sent to the cleaners. I have been lucky to find a dry cleaners in my area that does a ten piece special for a set price. I will accumulate items until I have ten and make a dry cleaner run to be sure I can get the special pricing.

Tips of the Trade

Clothing- Don't let small stains on clothing keep you from purchasing an item you love. I always carry a small pack of baby wipes to do a quick stain check. A lot of times, this will do the trick without damaging the material.

Woolite will be your new bestie when cleaning delicate vintage pieces. If the stain appears to be deeply soiled in the fabric, pour the detergent directly on the stain and massage it in with your fingers. Let it sit over night before handwashing. For stubborn stains, use a clean, soft-bristled toothbrush to gently work detergent into the area. Let the detergent sit for an hour and repeat. Make sure to work with the grain of the fabric. You must be gentle with vintage clothing because it may have delicate fibers that can break with excessive scrubbing. Wash on the gentle cycle and hang dry. White vinegar added to the wash will aid in neutralizing odors in your garments.

Jewelry- I am a jewelry counter junky! I have been lucky to score some unique pieces by staring down the jewelry counter. Here is how to get those jewels shining bright again.

Rubbing alcohol is my go to aid when cleaning and disinfecting jewelry. It's important to give thrifted jewelry the white glove treatment because you don't want to tarnish the finish on your costume jewelry. Pull out a few Q-tips along with some Dawn dishwashing soap and gently clean your pieces. I do take real gold and silver to my jeweler and they professionally clean my items for a small fee. It's a small price to pay when you've scored items at a fraction of the retail price.

Footwear – When you are looking to purchase shoes from a thrift store, there are a few tips to keep in mind. Check the soles and heels to make sure they aren't worn beyond simple repair. Also, check inside the shoe to see if there is mold or foot stains inside. Again, there is no amount of money worth saving in exchange for moldy feet.

Cut a dryer sheet in half and slip one half into each shoe to give your shoes a fresh boost. By keeping the dryer sheets in before wear, you can insure a fresh scent. Bananas are for more than just banana bread. Use the peel to rub off any scuff marks. The banana peel will leave a nice shine. The natural oils from the peel also make leather shoes more flexible. Spray the inside of the shoes with Lysol or other disinfectant spray to kill germs. Make sure you avoid spraying the outside of the shoe as it can damage the material.

Handbags- Handbags are an easy section to sort through, so you want to be sure you know how to properly clean and disinfect that Micheal Kors leather bag you can't wait to carry! Use a hand held vacuum or wand attachment on your vacuum cleaner to suck up any crumbs, lint, paper or other debris from the bottom of a thrift store purse. Baby wipes can be used to clean up small marks on the purse lining. Freshen the handbag by placing a dryer sheet inside. If the purse is leather or faux leather, make it shine by rubbing it with a banana peel.

Chapter 6

READY. SET. WEAR.

You've been to the local thrift store. You have your fabulous thrift finds washed and sanitized. Now what? Get ready to slay! Now it is time to have fun styling those new pieces and adding them to your wardrobe. I am including some style tips to enhance your thrift experience.

Style Tip #1: Find A Tailor

Make sure you have a tailor on speed dial. When discussing a great tailor, the possibilities are endless. A good tailor will be your bestie on your thrift journey! I actually have two different places that I use for alterations that require special attention. If you do not have a tailor on speed dial, dry cleaners are usually good places to take items in for a basic hem or button fix. For items that require a total overhaul, I use a real deal designer. I don't do this often because it can get a tad bit pricey. Nobody wants to pay $100 worth of alterations for a dress that only cost $2.00, but in some rare instances, I have done this. Judge me! Making sure items are well-tailored are the key to making your garments fit to perfection. A tailored look will give you an expensive look when executed correctly. Make sure your tailor is knowledgeable, skilled and detailed. In other words, make sure your tailor knows what he/she is doing!

Style Tip #2: Statement Pieces Really Do Make Statements

Accessorize your finds with a statement piece. I love an unexpected statement piece. The right pop of color can change your look from drab to fab with a simple addition of an item with flair. Dare to be different. You can decide what statement you are making, just make it well!

Style Tip #3: Don't Forget The Bling

If you are looking for an easy way to update your wardrobe, check out the thrift store jewelry selection. Most thrift stores have a large selection of jewelry ranging from watches to earrings. I find that vintage jewelry is difficult to distinguish. Vintage brooches and necklaces are my go to accessory when looking to change an outfit from basic to fabulous. Adding just the right piece can give you an expensive look for less.

The jewelry counter is one of my first stops on my thrifting treasure hunts and an easy place for a beginning thrifter to get their feet in the game. The jewelry section usually consists of four cases at the most. This gives an individual the opportunity to focus on that particular section and reduces a newbie's anxiety without the stress of thousands of clothing items on racks. Focusing on the jewelry section can really pay off. I remember going to the Goodwill with my mother. She started by browsing the jewelry counter while I gave the shoe section my attention. She didn't have much luck, so she walked over to the dress section. I then took my shot at the very same jewelry counter and scored by finding a small, dainty Gucci watch that my mom overlooked! Having a great eye and a little thrift luck was all I needed to uncover this treasure. When something is meant for you, it's meant for you! Train your senses to look for the bling. It may be shining right at you or it may be a diamond in the rough!

Style Tip #4: Don't Be Bound by the Belt

Change the belt. Vintage dresses and jumpsuits often come with the matching belts. Although this is a thrift score if all of the pieces come together, be sure to change out the belt on these items to update your look. I have been lucky enough to score some amazing vintage belts and some that needed a little bit of tender, loving care. Don't be afraid of a little rehab work. Spray paint can go a long way and create a completely different look.

Style Tip #5: Thrifting=DIY

Don't be afraid of a little DIY. Let those creative juices flow. It is ok to change up the buttons on a blazer or shorten the hem of an evening gown to give the garment new life. Small changes can update a look. Thrifting is all about "doing it yourself." You are finding the bargain. You are securing the deal. You are becoming a stylist. You are being introduced to fashion in an entirely new way. This is all about you. It may sound daunting, but you are the master of this game. There is beauty in that.

Style Tip #6: Have Fun!

I wouldn't introduce you to the #thriftlife if I didn't think it was fun. Yes, it is work and there is the thrill of the chase, but I had fun with my mom and I have fun when I am with my daughter. I have fun when I'm by myself. But more importantly, I want you to have fun and if you follow my advice, you just might!

As is all retail therapy, thrifting is cheaper than therapy sessions. I'm a wife, a mother, a teacher, a daughter, and a number of other roles I play and juggling all of those roles is hard. As women, we strive to do it all and we carry a lot on our plates. Stepping inside of those thrift stores is not just about finding a fabulous new dress, although that's a plus, it is about having a moment of peace and a moment of clarity. It is therapeutic for me to make a stop at the thrift store. I go in to clear my mind of all the stress that the day has created. On days when I need to decompress before picking up my kids, I seek solace inside of the thrift store. I am grateful for the outlet I have in thrifting and for the friends I have made in the world of thrifting. I am also thankful for the amazing fashions I have curated as a result of thrifting. After all, we look good, we feel good and when we feel good, we can conquer the world right?

Being a self-proclaimed Master Thrifter is something that won't happen overnight and just know that every time you step inside a thrift store, you will not always score fabulous finds. I have walked out of the store empty handed many times, and that is ok! My hope is that you now realize that you can play this game, win this game and master this game. Remember, anyone can wear clothes, but not everybody can be a fashionista!

See you in the world of thrifting!

My Favorite Thrift Stores

Here are a few of my favorite thrift stores in my area, as well as a few thrift bloggers that inspire me; I'm sure they will inspire you too.

Goodwill North Georgia

1460 Northside Drive NW, Atlanta, Georgia 30318
2100 Riverside Parkway, Lawrenceville, Georgia 30043

Finders Keepers Boutique

2134 N Decatur Road, Decatur, Georgia 30033

Labels Resale Boutique

3235 Paces Ferry Place NW, Atlanta, Georgia 30305

Follow these Thrift Style Influencers...

Talesha Austin- Diva Xpress @divaxpress
Multi-talented in the areas of thrifting and home décor. Talesha is the owner of an online store where she sells unique thrifted finds.

Tia Couture-Vintage Connoisseur @TiaCouture
Fashion Stylist specializing in high quality vintage pieces. Tia has great thrift style paired with high end pieces. I especially love her feminine pieces.

Sammy Davis- Thrift Boss Babes @sammydtv
Founder of Thrift Boss Babes. Sammy is a thrift, resale business coach based out of New York City.

Keren Duclosel- Thrifting Atlanta @twostylishkays
Founder of one of the largest thrifting groups on Facebook. Thrifting Atlanta showcases thrift style of women around the country. Keren inspires women to create stylish wardrobes on a budget.

Lauren McCray – True Lo Style @Truelostyle
Thrift style blogger and owner of True Lo Style. Lauren sells colorful and unique pieces. Based out of California, she certainly gives west coast vibes.

Ayanna Pitterson- Thrifting Divas @thriftingdivas
Social Media Influencer and thrifter. Ayanna uses her social media following to educate women on self care, money management and fashion slaying while maintaining a budget.

Ieshathegr8 - @thriftntell
Major thrifting content queen. Iesha uses her social media to produce great videos and runway looks direct from the thrift store!

Acknowledgements

I consider myself truly blessed. The realization of this book is simply added proof of that fact. God's voice and vision has been clear to me and while I have tried my hand in various projects, He has made it clear that the world of thrifting is truly my destiny. God, thank you.

To my husband, Tray- Thank you for being awesome. Thank you for listening to my earliest dreams about the book, thank you for your patience as I scribbled notes on napkins and post-it notes. Thank you for your advice on the cover design. Thank you for putting your engineering brain to work and helping me to think of every angle. Thank you for your unyielding support.

To my children, Toni and Trenton- Thank you for helping Mommy be creative. You give me such space to be free in the world. To Toni, my mini-fashionista. You have already begun to change the narrative and I enjoy learning from you. To Trenton, there is no love like a boy-mom love. To both of you, I can't wait to see what the future holds.

To my mother, Vickie Polite- You are the reason behind so many of my reasons. Thank you for stirring up this passion for thrifting. You have always been and continue to be my biggest cheerleader. You loved receiving *Essence* magazines and have always believed that one day, I would grace the pages. I believe we are on the way. Thank you for letting me style my dolls with the pages of your magazine. Thank you for fueling my creativity. Thank you for letting me thrive.

To my little sister, Jamina- Thank you for being my first personal styling client. Who knew that cutting up socks to style Barbie dolls would lead to a world of thrifting and styling?

To my brother, TJ- Thank you for your admiration. You've always looked at me like I can do anything and now I believe I can.

To my Dream Team, Lisa and April- Lisa, you have been encouraging me and pushing me for years. You helped me push this project to completion. I knew after trusting you with my wedding, I could trust you with anything. You operate in excellence! April, your words truly have power. I greatly appreciate your gift. I am indebted to the both of you as I watch my book come to fruition.

To Dad and Arlene- Thank you for your constant support and prayers. Arlene, you are a prayer warrior! Dad, you are my tech support and my business idea bouncer! I am grateful for your love always.

To my Thomas Family, to my Leslie Family, to my sorority sisters- the special ladies of Alpha Kappa Alpha Sorority, Incorporated, to my GNAC Jack and Jill Family and to my social media family. To Samantha Thomas and Karen Thomas, my cousins and very special styling clients. To Christina Brown- my assistant project manager and accountability partner- thank you for your faith in me. To Jewanna Porter- the best public relations manager in Atlanta. To Tamera Walker- thank you for the most amazing pep talks.

To Mom Maya, Mom Cherie and Mom Mavis- thank you for your support and ensuring I remain focused! To my thrifting sisters, Keren Duclosel and Ayanna Pitterson- thank you for opening your social media platforms to me so that I would have the opportunity to flourish. To Jonita Coleman and Nastassja Cockerell- thank you for the collaboration and the amazing thrift adventures.

To my glam squad- thank you for making sure that I always look amazing! My make up artists, D'Anna and Scoobie West. Tiffany, my wardrobe assistant, who always helps me to think outside of the box and create new clothing concepts. To DeWayne of Interscope Photography for capturing me perfectly and always clearing your schedule for me.

To you- my reader, my follower, my client and my friend. Thank you for trusting me enough to go on this journey with me. I could not have asked for a more amazing start. Thank you.

Talia

About the Author

Talia Leslie is a master at navigating the world of thrift stores. Armed with an eye for style, she understands the crossroads of designer shopping and bargain hunting. She has been passionate about finding the most stylish pieces at the best prices for over thirty years and her pursuit in the world of retail has earned her the name, "The High Low Fashionista." She truly believes that fashion and budget never have to be sacrificed in order to save the other.

Talia holds a Bachelors of Childhood Development from Fort Valley State University and is certified in Special Education. She has a fourteen year background and comprehensive career in education. Talia is also a dedicated member of the community, holding membership in both Alpha Kappa Alpha Sorority, Inc. and Jack and Jill of America, Inc.

When Talia is not "eyeing" her latest find, she is spending time with her family- comprised of her husband of eight years, Tray, and her two children, Toni and Trenton. They live outside of Atlanta, Georgia and enjoy living, learning and loving life.

@thehighlowfashionista
For booking, email thehighlowfashionista@gmail.com

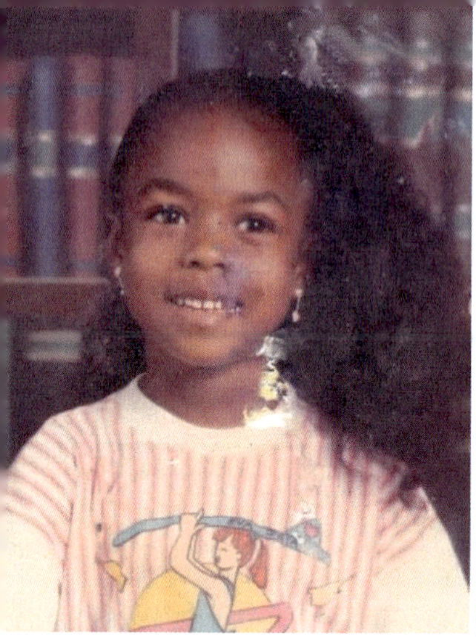

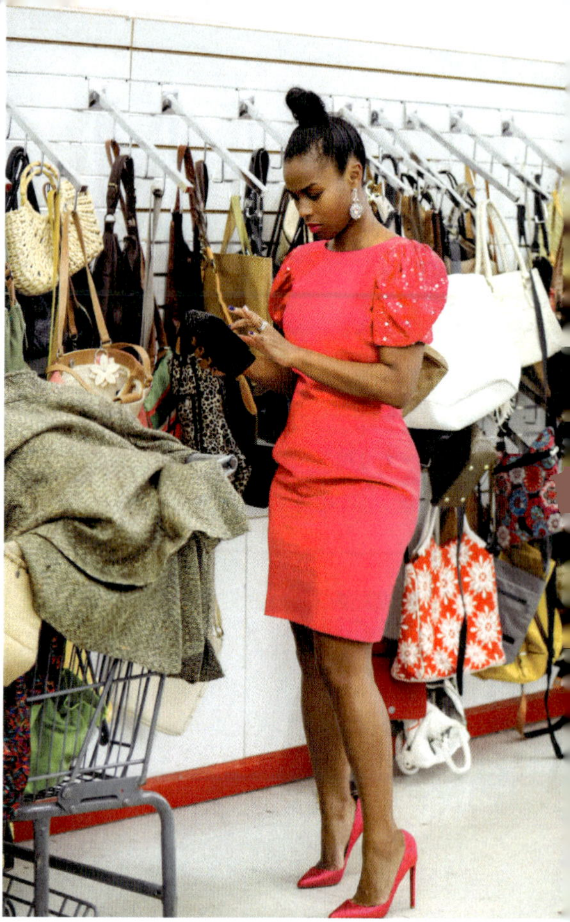

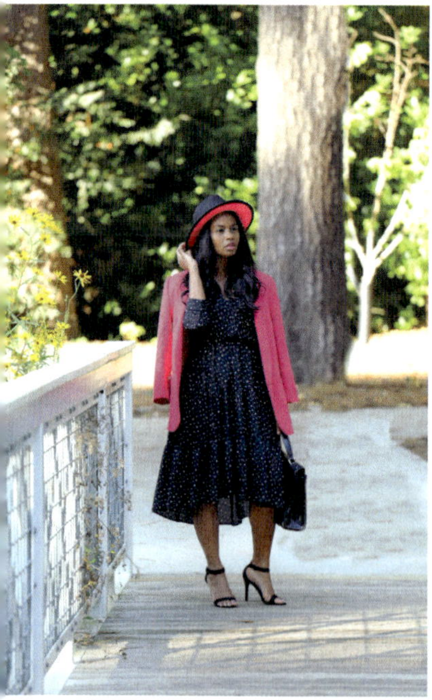

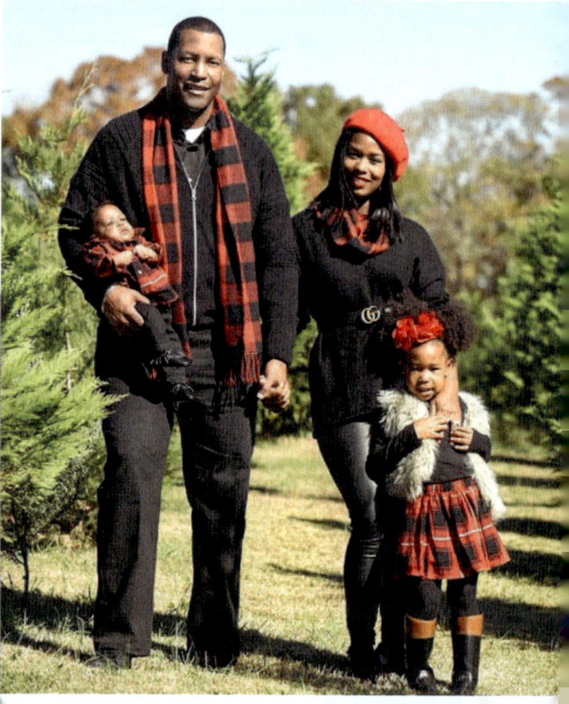

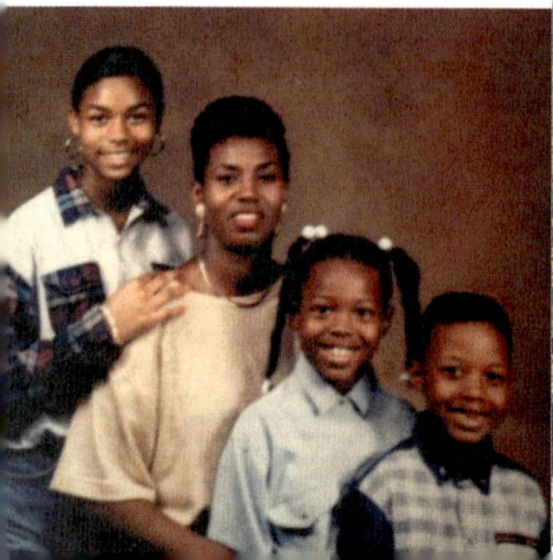

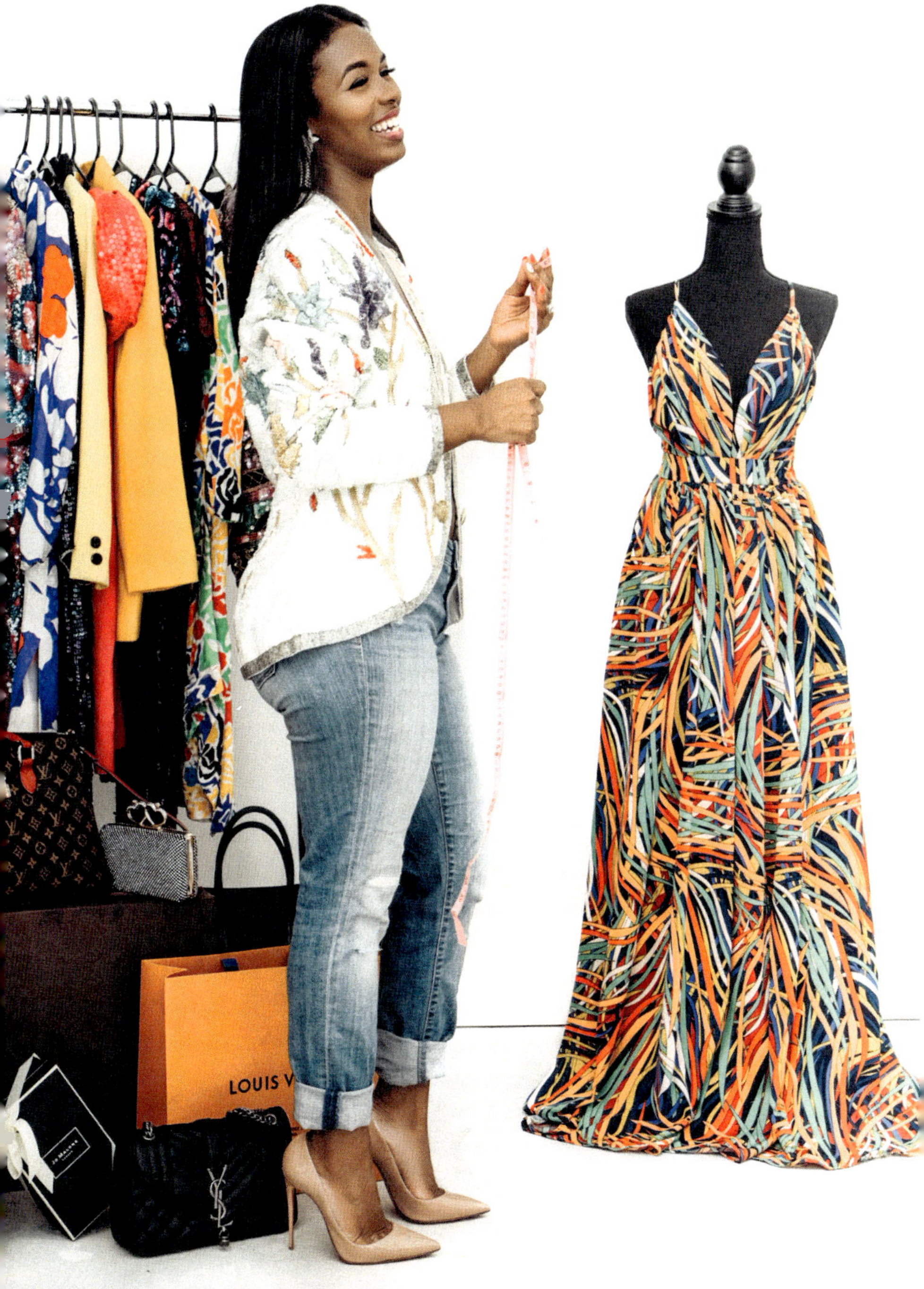
LOUIS V